Notes

Numbers in the text and tables may not add up to totals because of rounding.

Unless this report indicates otherwise, all years mentioned are federal fiscal years, which run from October 1 through September 30 and are designated by the calendar year in which they end.

Supplemental data for this analysis are available at CBO's website (www.cbo.gov/publication/ 51383), as is a glossary of common budgetary and economic terms (www.cbo.gov/publication/ 42904).

Contents

An Analysis of the President's 2017 Budget

Summary

This report by the Congressional Budget Office presents an analysis of the President's budget request for fiscal year 2017.[1] The analysis is based on CBO's economic projections and estimating models, rather than on the Administration's, and the estimates of the effects of the President's tax proposals were prepared by the staff of the Joint Committee on Taxation (JCT).[2] The economic projections used in this analysis largely reflect CBO's assessment of the effects of fiscal policies under current law. Later this year, in a separate report, CBO will analyze the full economic effects of the President's proposals and their implications for the federal budget.

Under the President's proposals, the federal budget deficit would decline in 2017 and 2018. After that, however, outlays would rise more quickly than revenues, so deficits would grow. As a result, federal debt held by the public would grow as well. By 2026—the end of the period covered by the President's budget—such debt would be higher than it is now, measured as a percentage of the nation's economic output, and it would be rising.

Deficits would be smaller under the President's proposals than those that would occur under current law, CBO projects—by a small amount for the current fiscal year and by larger amounts for the next 10 years. Most of that deficit reduction would be achieved by raising revenues.

Under the President's Proposals, Deficits Would Shrink Over the Next Two Years and Then Rise Steadily

Under the President's proposals, CBO estimates, the deficit would total $529 billion in 2016. It would fall to $433 billion in 2017, fall further to $383 billion in 2018, and then increase in most subsequent years, eventually growing to $972 billion in 2026 (see Table 1). The cumulative deficit over the 2017–2026 period would total $6.9 trillion. Measured as a percentage of output, the deficit would equal 2.9 percent of gross domestic product (GDP) in 2016, drop to about 2 percent for the next two years, and then start increasing; it would equal 3.5 percent in 2026. (The average deficit over the past 50 years has equaled 2.8 percent of GDP.)

Federal debt held by the public would equal 75 percent of GDP this year and next, dip to 74 percent for the following few years, and then start rising again. By the end of 2026, it would total $21.4 trillion, or 77 percent of GDP.

Deficits Would Be Smaller Under the President's Proposals Than Under Current Law

CBO estimates that the President's proposals would result in smaller deficits than those in the agency's baseline budget projections, which largely reflect the assumption that current tax and spending laws will remain unchanged.[3] This year, the proposals would reduce the deficit by $5 billion, mostly by changing policies affecting revenues. The deficit would remain lower than projected in the baseline during every year of the 2017–2026 period,

1. CBO has analyzed the budget that the Administration submitted to the Congress on February 9, 2016, as well as a supplemental request for funds to respond to the Zika virus, which was made on February 22.

2. For more details about the President's tax proposals, see Joint Committee on Taxation, *Estimated Budget Effects of the Revenue Provisions Contained in the President's Fiscal Year 2017 Budget Proposal*, JCX-15-16 (March 24, 2016), http://go.usa.gov/cAX7j (PDF, 96 KB).

3. CBO regularly produces such projections, which serve as a benchmark against which the President's proposals and other potential legislation can be measured. For the latest projections, see Congressional Budget Office, *Updated Budget Projections: 2016 to 2026* (March 2016), www.cbo.gov/publication/51384. Those projections incorporate the effects of legislation enacted through March 4, 2016. For CBO's previous budget projections, as well as the agency's assessment of the economic outlook, see Congressional Budget Office, *The Budget and Economic Outlook: 2016 to 2026* (January 2016), www.cbo.gov/publication/51129.

Table 1.

Comparison of Projected Revenues, Outlays, and Deficits in CBO's Baseline and Under the President's Budget

Billions of Dollars

	Actual, 2015	2016	2017	2018	2019	2020	2021	2022	2023	2024	2025	2026	Total 2017-2021	2017-2026
CBO's March 2016 Baseline														
Revenues	3,250	3,364	3,508	3,645	3,772	3,931	4,082	4,247	4,423	4,615	4,825	5,042	18,937	42,089
Outlays	3,688	3,897	4,058	4,194	4,482	4,729	4,972	5,290	5,504	5,709	6,051	6,385	22,434	51,373
Deficit	**-438**	**-534**	**-550**	**-549**	**-710**	**-798**	**-890**	**-1,043**	**-1,080**	**-1,094**	**-1,226**	**-1,343**	**-3,497**	**-9,283**
CBO's Estimate of the President's Budget														
Revenues	3,250	3,369	3,672	3,871	4,035	4,205	4,377	4,541	4,713	4,920	5,155	5,395	20,161	44,885
Outlays	3,688	3,897	4,105	4,254	4,554	4,790	5,028	5,332	5,539	5,733	6,072	6,367	22,732	51,774
Deficit	**-438**	**-529**	**-433**	**-383**	**-518**	**-585**	**-651**	**-791**	**-826**	**-813**	**-917**	**-972**	**-2,571**	**-6,889**
Difference Between CBO's Estimate of the President's Budget and CBO's Baseline														
Revenues	n.a.	5	164	226	264	275	296	294	289	305	330	353	1,224	2,795
Outlays	n.a.	*	48	61	72	61	56	42	35	24	21	-18	298	401
Deficit[a]	**n.a.**	**5**	**116**	**165**	**192**	**213**	**240**	**252**	**254**	**281**	**309**	**372**	**926**	**2,394**
Memorandum:														
Deficit as a Percentage of GDP														
CBO's baseline	-2.5	-2.9	-2.8	-2.7	-3.4	-3.7	-3.9	-4.4	-4.4	-4.3	-4.6	-4.9	-3.3	-4.0
CBO's estimate of the President's budget	-2.5	-2.9	-2.2	-1.9	-2.5	-2.7	-2.9	-3.4	-3.4	-3.2	-3.5	-3.5	-2.5	-3.0
Debt Held by the Public as a Percentage of GDP														
CBO's baseline	73.6	75.4	75.5	75.4	76.2	77.2	78.3	79.8	81.2	82.4	83.9	85.6	n.a.	n.a.
CBO's estimate of the President's budget	73.6	75.4	74.9	74.1	74.1	74.3	74.4	75.0	75.7	76.1	76.7	77.4	n.a.	n.a.

Sources: Congressional Budget Office; staff of the Joint Committee on Taxation.

GDP = gross domestic product; n.a. = not applicable; * = between zero and $500 million.

a. Positive numbers indicate a decrease in the deficit in relation to CBO's baseline.

resulting in a cumulative deficit that was $2.4 trillion less than the $9.3 trillion projected in the baseline. Deficits over the period would average 3.0 percent of GDP, or 1.0 percentage point lower than their average in the baseline (see Figure 1). As a consequence, debt held by the public would also be lower than projected in the baseline—by 2026, about 8 percentage points of GDP lower (see Figure 2).

The President's proposals would achieve most of that deficit reduction by increasing revenues. Between 2017 and 2026, revenues would be $2.8 trillion (or 7 percent) higher than in CBO's baseline projections. The proposals that would result in the largest increases in revenues are the following:

- Limiting certain individual income tax deductions for higher-income taxpayers ($543 billion);

- Enacting immigration reform ($386 billion);[4]

- Imposing a minimum tax on certain foreign income ($298 billion);

- Imposing a tax on oil ($273 billion); and

- Increasing taxes on capital gains and dividends ($245 billion).

---

4. The proposal to enact immigration reform would also increase outlays by $285 billion over the 2017–2026 period, CBO and JCT estimate; it would thus have the net effect of reducing deficits by $101 billion.

Figure 1.

Deficits Projected in CBO's Baseline and Under the President's Budget

Percentage of Gross Domestic Product

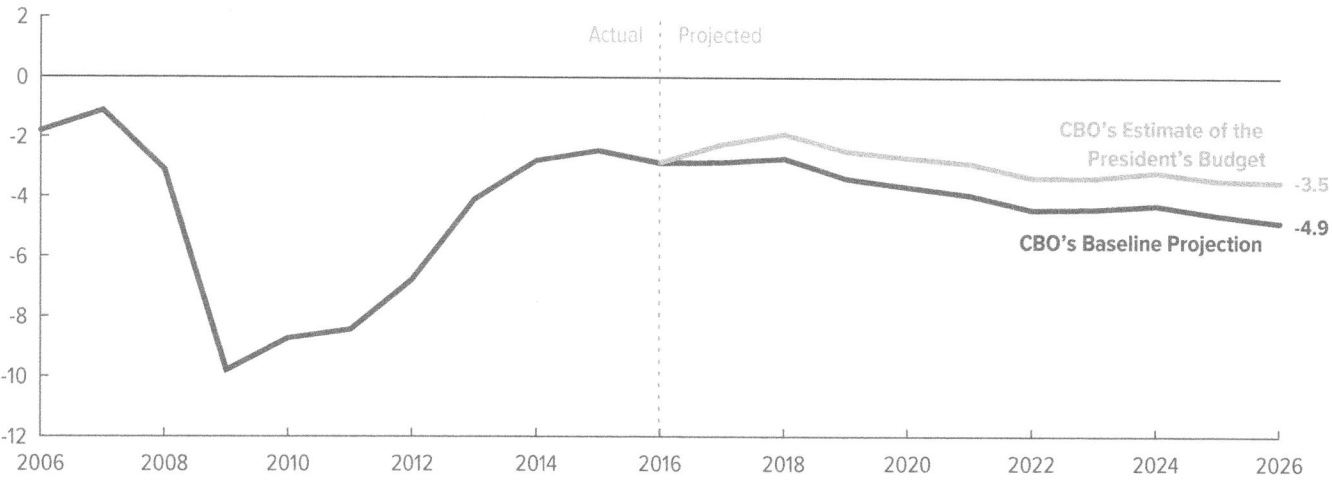

Source: Congressional Budget Office.

Under the President's proposals, total revenues would equal 19.3 percent of GDP from 2017 through 2026, on average (see Table 2). In the baseline, by contrast, revenues are projected to average 18.1 percent of GDP during that period. Over the past 50 years, they have averaged 17.4 percent.

In most years, total outlays would also be higher under the President's proposals than in the baseline, though the difference would be much smaller than for revenues—less than $1 billion higher this year and $401 billion (or 1 percent) higher over the 2017–2026 period. The 10-year increase would be the net result of the following changes:

■ An increase of $1.0 trillion in mandatory spending (which is spending for programs generally governed by provisions of permanent law)—consisting of a $1.4 trillion increase in spending related to immigration reform, income security programs, transportation, education, and other areas, offset in part by a $0.4 trillion reduction in Medicare outlays;[5]

■ A decrease of $288 billion in discretionary outlays (which result from funding provided or controlled by

appropriation acts)—stemming from sharply lower outlays for military operations and related activities in Afghanistan and elsewhere (known as overseas contingency operations, or OCO) and from a reclassification of some transportation spending, partially offset by an increase in other discretionary outlays; and

■ A decrease of $343 billion in net interest costs, primarily the result of the lower deficits that would occur under the President's proposals.

Under the proposals, total outlays would average 22.3 percent of GDP from 2017 to 2026. In CBO's baseline, they average 22.1 percent of GDP during that period. They have averaged 20.2 percent of GDP over the past 50 years.

CBO's Estimates of Deficits Under the President's Proposals Are Mostly Higher Than the Administration's

CBO's estimate of the cumulative 10-year deficit under the President's proposals is $776 billion higher than the Administration's estimate of $6.1 trillion. Specifically, CBO's estimates of revenues are $1.6 trillion (or 4 percent) lower than the Administration's, and CBO's estimates of outlays are $856 billion (or 2 percent) lower. According to CBO's calculations, the deficit would be smaller than the Administration anticipates this year and for the following three years. After that, CBO estimates larger deficits under the President's policies than the Administration does.

---

5. One of the President's proposals that would increase spending would cancel automatic reductions to mandatory spending. Canceling those scheduled reductions would increase outlays for Medicare by $98 billion over the 2017–2026 period. That amount is included in the $1.4 trillion increase described here and is not reflected in the $0.4 trillion Medicare reduction.

Figure 2.

Federal Debt Held by the Public Projected in CBO's Baseline and Under the President's Budget

Percentage of Gross Domestic Product

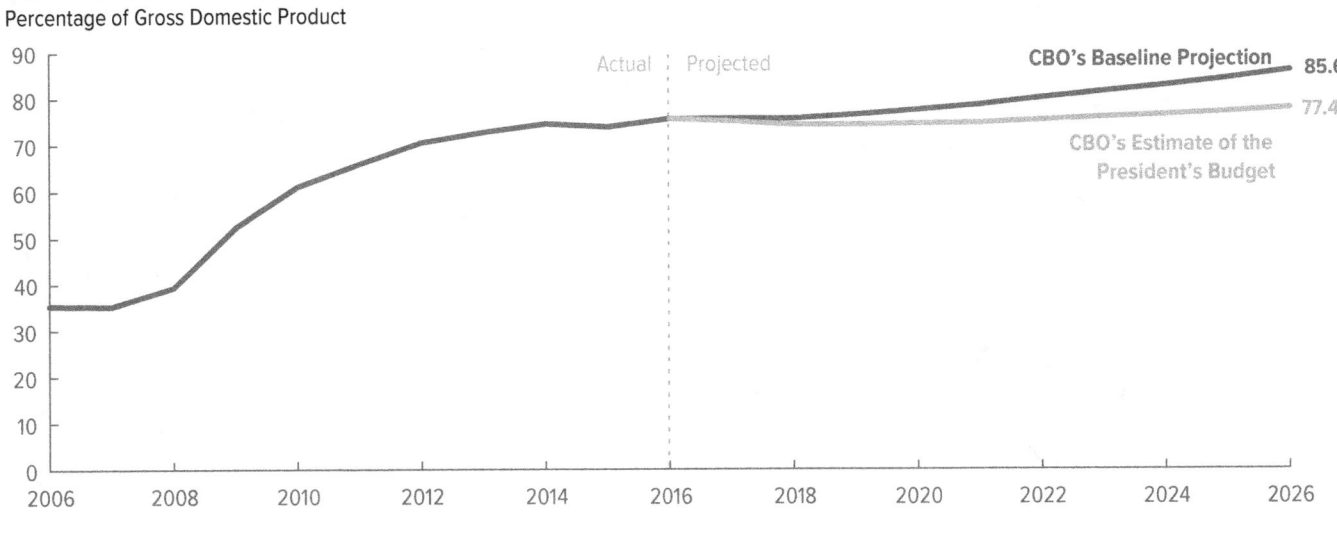

Source: Congressional Budget Office.

Of the $776 billion difference, roughly one-third stems from technical estimating differences, and about two-thirds is accounted for by variations between CBO's and the Administration's economic projections. Some of those variations arise because the Administration incorporates its assessment of the economic effects that the President's proposals would have; CBO's estimates, by contrast, are based on an economic forecast that reflects current law, except for some of the effects of the changes in the population and labor force that would result from the President's proposed immigration reform.[6]

Effects of the President's Proposals on the Budget

In 2016, the President's policy proposals would result in a $529 billion deficit, CBO and JCT estimate—$5 billion lower than the deficit that CBO estimates under current law. In each year between 2017 and 2026, according to CBO and JCT's estimates, the increase in revenues from enacting the President's proposals would exceed the corresponding change in outlays, thereby reducing the deficit in relation to the baseline. The cumulative deficit from 2017 through 2026 would be reduced by $2.4 trillion, or 26 percent.

6. The proposed immigration reform would affect the economy more directly than most proposals would; by increasing the size of the labor force and changing the legal status of some current workers, it would result in significantly higher receipts from income and payroll taxes. Therefore, CBO's analysis includes that effect on revenues, as did the agency's cost estimate for similar immigration legislation that was considered in 2013.

Proposals That Would Affect Revenues

The President's proposals include a number of changes to laws that would affect revenues. If enacted, CBO and JCT estimate, those changes would make revenues $2.8 trillion (or 7 percent) higher over the 2017–2026 period than in the baseline (see Table 3).[7] (Many of those proposals would also affect outlays. For example, they would boost outlays for certain refundable tax credits— the earned income tax credit, the child tax credit, and the American Opportunity Tax Credit, or AOTC—by $114 billion between 2017 and 2026, as the section below on mandatory spending explains.)[8]

7. The President's 2017 budget contains an extensive set of proposals called "elements of business tax reform" that would increase revenues by $530 billion over 10 years, JCT estimates. Those proposals include imposing a minimum 19 percent tax on foreign income, making additional changes to U.S. international tax law, and repealing the "last-in, first-out" method of accounting for inventories. Although the President's budget also discusses the Administration's goal of cutting the corporate tax rate as part of a framework for business tax reform, it contains no specific proposal or estimate of a revenue effect for such a cut. Therefore, in CBO's analysis of the President's proposals, the agency has included the $530 billion revenue increase but no revenue reductions from corporate tax rate cuts.

8. Tax credits reduce a taxpayer's overall income tax liability; if a refundable credit exceeds a taxpayer's other income tax liabilities, all or a portion of the excess (depending on the particular credit) is refunded to the taxpayer, and that payment is recorded as an outlay in the budget.

Table 2.

CBO's Estimate of the President's Budget

	Actual, 2015	2016	2017	2018	2019	2020	2021	2022	2023	2024	2025	2026	Total 2017-2021	Total 2017-2026
	In Billions of Dollars													
Revenues														
On-budget	2,480	2,574	2,843	3,004	3,131	3,267	3,407	3,531	3,667	3,831	4,027	4,221	15,652	34,928
Off-budget[a]	770	794	829	867	904	938	971	1,010	1,046	1,089	1,128	1,174	4,509	9,957
Total	**3,250**	**3,369**	**3,672**	**3,871**	**4,035**	**4,205**	**4,377**	**4,541**	**4,713**	**4,920**	**5,155**	**5,395**	**20,161**	**44,885**
Outlays														
Mandatory	2,297	2,449	2,582	2,687	2,907	3,074	3,247	3,485	3,623	3,754	4,020	4,244	14,497	33,623
Discretionary	1,168	1,196	1,219	1,207	1,222	1,234	1,252	1,270	1,287	1,305	1,336	1,361	6,133	12,692
Net interest	223	252	304	360	425	482	530	577	628	673	717	762	2,102	5,458
Total	**3,688**	**3,897**	**4,105**	**4,254**	**4,554**	**4,790**	**5,028**	**5,332**	**5,539**	**5,733**	**6,072**	**6,367**	**22,732**	**51,774**
On-budget	2,945	3,124	3,291	3,390	3,631	3,803	3,973	4,202	4,331	4,444	4,696	4,896	18,088	40,657
Off-budget[a]	743	774	815	864	923	987	1,055	1,130	1,207	1,289	1,377	1,471	4,644	11,117
Deficit (-) or Surplus	**-438**	**-529**	**-433**	**-383**	**-518**	**-585**	**-651**	**-791**	**-826**	**-813**	**-917**	**-972**	**-2,571**	**-6,889**
On-budget	-466	-550	-447	-386	-500	-536	-566	-671	-665	-614	-669	-675	-2,436	-5,730
Off-budget[a]	27	21	14	3	-19	-48	-85	-120	-161	-200	-248	-297	-134	-1,160
Debt Held by the Public	13,117	13,946	14,454	14,906	15,484	16,121	16,818	17,656	18,532	19,402	20,379	21,417	n.a.	n.a.
Memorandum:														
Gross Domestic Product[b]	17,810	18,494	19,297	20,127	20,906	21,710	22,593	23,528	24,497	25,506	26,559	27,660	104,632	232,382
	As a Percentage of Gross Domestic Product													
Revenues														
On-budget	13.9	13.9	14.7	14.9	15.0	15.0	15.1	15.0	15.0	15.0	15.2	15.3	15.0	15.0
Off-budget[a]	4.3	4.3	4.3	4.3	4.3	4.3	4.3	4.3	4.3	4.3	4.2	4.2	4.3	4.3
Total	**18.2**	**18.2**	**19.0**	**19.2**	**19.3**	**19.4**	**19.4**	**19.3**	**19.2**	**19.3**	**19.4**	**19.5**	**19.3**	**19.3**
Outlays														
Mandatory	12.9	13.2	13.4	13.4	13.9	14.2	14.4	14.8	14.8	14.7	15.1	15.3	13.9	14.5
Discretionary	6.6	6.5	6.3	6.0	5.8	5.7	5.5	5.4	5.3	5.1	5.0	4.9	5.9	5.5
Net interest	1.3	1.4	1.6	1.8	2.0	2.2	2.3	2.5	2.6	2.6	2.7	2.8	2.0	2.3
Total	**20.7**	**21.1**	**21.3**	**21.1**	**21.8**	**22.1**	**22.3**	**22.7**	**22.6**	**22.5**	**22.9**	**23.0**	**21.7**	**22.3**
On-budget	16.5	16.9	17.1	16.8	17.4	17.5	17.6	17.9	17.7	17.4	17.7	17.7	17.3	17.5
Off-budget[a]	4.2	4.2	4.2	4.3	4.4	4.5	4.7	4.8	4.9	5.1	5.2	5.3	4.4	4.8
Deficit (-) or Surplus	**-2.5**	**-2.9**	**-2.2**	**-1.9**	**-2.5**	**-2.7**	**-2.9**	**-3.4**	**-3.4**	**-3.2**	**-3.5**	**-3.5**	**-2.5**	**-3.0**
On-budget	-2.6	-3.0	-2.3	-1.9	-2.4	-2.5	-2.5	-2.9	-2.7	-2.4	-2.5	-2.4	-2.3	-2.5
Off-budget[a]	0.2	0.1	0.1	*	-0.1	-0.2	-0.4	-0.5	-0.7	-0.8	-0.9	-1.1	-0.1	-0.5
Debt Held by the Public	73.6	75.4	74.9	74.1	74.1	74.3	74.4	75.0	75.7	76.1	76.7	77.4	n.a.	n.a.

Sources: Congressional Budget Office; staff of the Joint Committee on Taxation.

n.a. = not applicable; * = between zero and 0.05 percent.

a. The revenues and outlays of the Social Security trust funds and the net cash flow of the Postal Service are classified as off-budget.

b. These estimates come from CBO's baseline economic projections and do not reflect the macroeconomic effects of the President's proposals.

Table 3.

CBO's Estimate of the Effects of the President's Budget Proposals

Billions of Dollars

	2016	2017	2018	2019	2020	2021	2022	2023	2024	2025	2026	Total 2017-2021	Total 2017-2026
Deficit in CBO's March 2016 Baseline	-534	-550	-549	-710	-798	-890	-1,043	-1,080	-1,094	-1,226	-1,343	-3,497	-9,283
Effects of the President's Proposals													
Revenues													
Limit certain tax deductions and exclusions	-1	14	51	49	52	55	58	61	64	67	71	222	543
Enact immigration reform	0	1	10	25	30	35	40	50	55	65	75	101	386
Impose a minimum tax on foreign income earned after 2016	0	13	32	35	33	31	31	30	30	31	31	144	298
Impose a tax on oil	0	6	10	16	22	28	35	38	39	40	40	81	273
Increase taxes on capital gains and dividends	4	22	4	20	22	23	26	28	30	33	36	92	245
Expand the base for the net investment income tax and self-employment payroll taxes	0	14	21	22	23	24	24	25	26	28	29	103	236
Impose a onetime tax on certain accumulated foreign earnings	0	61	53	33	37	40	14	-13	-12	-10	-9	224	195
Modify estate and gift taxes	0	1	10	12	15	18	20	22	24	27	30	56	178
Other proposals	2	31	36	52	42	41	46	47	48	49	50	201	441
Total Effect on Revenues	**5**	**164**	**226**	**264**	**275**	**296**	**294**	**289**	**305**	**330**	**353**	**1,224**	**2,795**
Outlays													
Mandatory													
Make changes to Medicare	0	-2	-9	-20	-31	-37	-43	-47	-53	-64	-72	-99	-376
Enact immigration reform	0	5	10	15	20	25	30	35	40	50	55	75	285
Increase funding for income security	0	7	13	19	23	27	29	31	33	37	43	89	262
Reclassify and increase spending for transportation programs	0	3	8	15	23	30	36	37	36	33	28	80	250
Increase funding for education and job training	0	1	6	10	14	16	17	19	24	30	32	46	168
Increase funding for Medicaid and other health programs	*	10	13	20	17	15	13	14	13	13	12	128	140
Modify refundable tax credits	0	*	11	12	12	13	13	13	13	13	14	48	114
Cancel automatic spending reductions[a]	0	7	9	11	12	12	13	14	14	22	*	51	113
Other proposals	0	4	3	3	4	6	7	9	12	14	14	20	76
Subtotal, mandatory	*	36	63	85	95	107	115	125	132	148	126	386	1,033

Continued

Limit Certain Tax Deductions and Exclusions. The President proposes to limit the extent to which higher-income taxpayers can reduce their tax liability through certain deductions and exclusions by capping the reduction in tax liability at 28 percent of the value of those deductions and exclusions. That change would increase revenues by $543 billion from 2017 to 2026, according to JCT.

Enact Immigration Reform. The President proposes to alter laws related to immigration, taking an approach similar to the one in immigration legislation that the Senate passed in 2013 (the Border Security, Economic Opportunity, and Immigration Modernization Act, S. 744). After adjusting CBO's cost estimate for that legislation to reflect changes in the baseline budget projections that have been made since 2013, and after taking into account other changes to the tax code proposed by the President, CBO and JCT project that the immigration proposal would increase revenues by $386 billion over the coming decade. (CBO and JCT also estimate that the proposal would increase mandatory spending by $285 billion over the same period; that increase is discussed in the section on mandatory spending.)[9]

---

9. For more information on how CBO and JCT estimate the effects of immigration reform proposals, see Congressional Budget Office, *How Changes in Immigration Policy Might Affect the Federal Budget* (January 2015), www.cbo.gov/publication/49868, and cost estimate for S. 744, the Border Security, Economic Opportunity, and Immigration Modernization Act (June 18, 2013), www.cbo.gov/publication/44225.

Table 3. Continued

CBO's Estimate of the Effects of the President's Budget Proposals

Billions of Dollars

	2016	2017	2018	2019	2020	2021	2022	2023	2024	2025	2026	Total 2017-2021	Total 2017-2026
Effects of the President's Proposals (Continued)													
Outlays													
Discretionary													
Reduce spending for overseas contingency operations	0	-1	-35	-51	-60	-65	-74	-79	-82	-85	-87	-212	-619
Reclassify transportation spending as mandatory	0	-2	-3	-3	-4	-4	-5	-5	-5	-5	-5	-16	-41
Other proposals	*	17	39	54	49	46	41	39	34	29	24	205	372
Subtotal, discretionary	*	14	2	-1	-14	-24	-38	-45	-53	-61	-68	-23	-288
Net interest	*	-1	-5	-12	-19	-27	-36	-45	-55	-65	-77	-65	-343
Total Effect on Outlays	*	**48**	**61**	**72**	**61**	**56**	**42**	**35**	**24**	**21**	**-18**	**298**	**401**
Total Effect on the Deficit[b]	**5**	**116**	**165**	**192**	**213**	**240**	**252**	**254**	**281**	**309**	**372**	**926**	**2,394**
Deficit Under the President's Budget as Estimated by CBO	-529	-433	-383	-518	-585	-651	-791	-826	-813	-917	-972	-2,571	-6,889
Memorandum:													
Total Effect on Noninterest Outlays	*	49	65	84	80	83	78	80	79	87	59	362	744

Sources: Congressional Budget Office; staff of the Joint Committee on Taxation.

* = between -$500 million and $500 million.

a. Refers to the reductions in automatic spending established by the Budget Control Act of 2011 and later amended. Automatic spending reductions to mandatory programs (known as sequestration) would be canceled under the President's budget for each year from 2016 to 2025 (the last year such reductions are in effect under current law).

b. Positive numbers indicate a decrease in the deficit in relation to CBO's baseline.

Impose a Minimum Tax on Foreign Income Earned After 2016. The President proposes a 19 percent minimum tax on the foreign income of U.S. corporations and of foreign corporations controlled by U.S. shareholders. The tax would be applied to foreign earnings in the year they were earned, starting in 2017; it would apply separately in each country where the corporation had earnings, and it would be reduced to account for foreign taxes paid. No further tax would be due when the foreign earnings were repatriated to the United States. Certain types of foreign income that are already automatically taxed in the year earned would continue to be taxed at the full U.S. statutory rate, which is generally higher than 19 percent. JCT estimates that the proposal would increase revenues by $298 billion over the 2017–2026 period.

Impose a Tax on Oil. The President proposes a new tax on domestically produced and imported petroleum products at a rate equivalent to $10.25 per barrel of crude oil. The tax would be phased in by equal amounts over five years, and it would be indexed for inflation. Exported petroleum products would be permanently exempt, and home heating oil would be temporarily exempt. JCT

estimates that the proposal would increase revenues by $273 billion over the 2017–2026 period.

Increase Taxes on Capital Gains and Dividends. The President proposes to increase the tax rates on capital gains and qualified dividends for higher-income taxpayers from 23.8 percent to 28.0 percent (including the existing 3.8 percent tax on net investment income). The President further proposes to tax the capital gains on certain assets transferred by gift or death if those gains are above a specified threshold. JCT estimates that the changes would increase revenues by $245 billion between 2017 and 2026.

Expand the Base for the Net Investment Income Tax and Self-Employment Payroll Taxes. The President proposes to expand the tax bases for both the 3.8 percent net investment income tax that applies to higher-income taxpayers and the Social Security and Medicare payroll taxes that apply to self-employed workers. The first of those taxes would be newly applied to the net business income (or loss) allocated to S corporation owners and limited partners. The payroll taxes would be newly applied, most significantly, to the net business income (or loss) allocated to owners of S corporations and certain limited partners in professional-services industries. That change would increase revenues by $236 billion from 2017 to 2026, according to JCT.

Impose a Onetime Tax on Certain Accumulated Foreign Earnings. Under the President's proposals, a onetime tax of 14 percent would be imposed on the accumulated earnings of foreign corporations controlled by U.S. shareholders. Only earnings that were not previously subject to U.S. taxation would face the tax, and a tax credit would be allowed for a portion of the income taxes paid to foreign governments on those earnings. No additional U.S. tax would be levied on those earnings if they were later repatriated to the United States. JCT estimates that the proposal would increase revenues by $195 billion over the 2017–2026 period.

Modify Estate and Gift Taxes. Starting in 2017, the parameters used to determine estate taxes, gift taxes, and generation-skipping transfer taxes (which apply to wealth transferred to an heir who is more than one generation younger) would be restored to their 2009 levels. The maximum tax rate applied to estates and gifts would thus rise to 45 percent, the amounts of wealth excluded from those taxes would decline, and those excluded amounts would no longer be indexed for inflation. Those changes, along with some others, would increase revenues by $178 billion over the 2017–2026 period, JCT estimates.

Other Revenue Proposals. Other proposals in the President's budget would, on net, increase revenues by $441 billion over the 10-year period. Proposals that would raise revenues include some other changes to U.S. international tax law ($134 billion); a fee on certain large banks and financial firms ($111 billion); a repeal of the "last-in, first-out" method of accounting for inventories ($107 billion); and an increase in tobacco taxes ($78 billion). Of proposals that would reduce revenues and partly offset the increases just mentioned, the most significant would be a second-earner tax credit ($79 billion).

Proposals That Would Affect Mandatory Spending

Over the 2017–2026 period, mandatory outlays would be higher under the President's proposals than under current law. An increase of $1.4 trillion for mandatory spending related to immigration reform and for income security programs, transportation, education, and other areas would be offset by a reduction of $0.4 trillion in Medicare outlays; that $0.4 trillion does not include the effects on Medicare of a separate proposal of the

President's—canceling automatic reductions in mandatory spending (see Table 3). All told, mandatory spending would be $1.0 trillion (or 3 percent) higher than projected in the baseline, according to CBO's estimates. Mandatory outlays under the President's budget would equal 13.4 percent of GDP in 2017 and grow to 15.3 percent by 2026; in CBO's baseline, they are 13.2 percent and 14.9 percent, respectively.

Make Changes to Medicare. The Administration proposes numerous changes to the laws governing Medicare, which together would reduce mandatory spending (net of offsetting receipts) by $376 billion from 2017 through 2026, CBO estimates.[10] (That amount does not include the effects on Medicare spending of the President's proposal to cancel automatic reductions in mandatory spending, which is discussed separately below.)

Most of the proposals affecting Medicare would decrease spending for the program over the 10-year period. The largest savings would result from the following proposals:

- Requiring manufacturers to pay rebates to the federal government on prescription drugs dispensed to low-income beneficiaries who are enrolled in Part D of Medicare ($134 billion);

- Reducing payments to post–acute care providers ($72 billion);

- Increasing premiums for some beneficiaries under Parts B and D of Medicare ($39 billion);

- Reducing Medicare's coverage of bad debts that result from beneficiaries' failure to pay deductibles, coinsurance, or both ($34 billion); and

- Restructuring Medicare Advantage payments ($26 billion).

A few proposals would increase Medicare spending over the 2017–2026 period, including eliminating the lifetime limit on inpatient services at psychiatric facilities ($3 billion) and no longer requiring beneficiaries to pay coinsurance for certain colonoscopies ($2 billion).

---

10. Offsetting receipts for Medicare include premiums paid by beneficiaries and recoveries of overpayments to providers, as well as payments by states for a portion of the cost of prescription drugs for low-income beneficiaries; those receipts are recorded in the budget as reductions in outlays.

Enact Immigration Reform. The President proposes to enact immigration reform similar to legislation that passed the Senate in 2013. For the purposes of this analysis, CBO and JCT have modified their estimates of spending and revenues for that legislation to reflect subsequent changes to baseline projections, including changes to average per capita benefits for certain programs, and also to reflect the additional costs that would accrue because of the President's proposed changes to refundable tax credits (which are described below). CBO and JCT estimate that enacting such a proposal would increase mandatory outlays by $285 billion from 2017 through 2026, mostly for refundable tax credits, health insurance subsidies offered under the Affordable Care Act, and Medicaid benefits. (In addition, CBO and JCT estimate that enacting comprehensive immigration reform would increase revenues by $386 billion.)

Increase Funding for Income Security. The President's proposals would increase outlays for income security by $262 billion. (That sum does not include the effects of proposed changes to refundable tax credits, which are discussed separately below.) The proposals that would have the largest budgetary effects, CBO estimates, are the following:

- Expanding access to child care ($78 billion);

- Establishing a family energy assistance fund ($65 billion);

- Creating a program to provide wage insurance ($28 billion);

- Increasing benefits and coverage under the Federal-State Unemployment Insurance Program ($26 billion);

- Increasing funds to assist the homeless ($19 billion);

- Increasing funds for nutrition programs ($18 billion);

- Providing more resources for foster care and other activities for children's welfare ($12 billion); and

- Increasing funding provided to states for the Temporary Assistance for Needy Families program ($10 billion).

Reclassify and Increase Spending for Transportation Programs. The President proposes to increase mandatory spending for transportation programs by $250 billion as part of his 21st Century Clean Transportation initiative.[11]

Of that amount, $209 billion would fund new transportation projects and research. In addition, outlays for certain existing transportation programs would be classified as mandatory rather than discretionary spending. That reclassification would increase mandatory outlays by $41 billion over the 2017–2026 period (and reduce discretionary outlays by the same amount, thus having no net budgetary impact).

Increase Funding for Education and Job Training. The President's proposals would increase mandatory spending for education and job training by $168 billion over the next decade, CBO estimates. That total includes $71 billion for preschool, elementary, and secondary education programs, $67 billion that would mostly help pay the costs of community college for some students, $38 billion for the Federal Pell Grant Program, and $12 billion for apprenticeship and job training programs. Some other proposals would increase or decrease spending for education and job training by smaller amounts.

Increase Funding for Medicaid and Other Health Programs. Proposed changes to health programs other than Medicare—including Medicaid, the Children's Health Insurance Program (CHIP), and the programs administered by the Health Resources and Services Administration—would boost mandatory spending by $140 billion, on net, from 2017 through 2026, CBO estimates. Of the proposals that would raise outlays, the following would have the largest effects:

- Reimbursing states that expand their Medicaid programs under provisions of the Affordable Care Act, regardless of the year in which they do so, for 100 percent of their additional Medicaid costs for three years, before phasing down that compensation ($31 billion);

- Increasing federal funding for Medicaid in Puerto Rico and other U.S. territories ($28 billion);

- Giving states the option to provide 12 months of continuous Medicaid coverage to adults regardless of changes in their circumstances ($18 billion);

- Expanding the Maternal, Infant, and Early Childhood Home Visiting program ($10 billion);

---

11. The programs affected by the proposal would be administered by the Department of Transportation, the Department of Energy, the Environmental Protection Agency, and the National Aeronautics and Space Administration.

■ Funding a pilot program for the provision of long-term care ($10 billion);

■ Continuing the increased funding provided under the Affordable Care Act for community health centers and the National Health Service Corps ($10 billion);

■ Increasing Medicaid's payment rates for primary care providers through 2017 ($9 billion); and

■ Funding CHIP, which is not currently funded beyond 2017, through 2019 ($6 billion).[12]

Other proposals, including the following, would reduce outlays:

■ Increasing rebates paid to the government by pharmaceutical companies for drugs purchased through Medicaid ($7 billion);

■ Requiring remittances from Medicaid and CHIP managed care plans for costs that exceed a minimum medical loss ratio ($6 billion);[13] and

■ Reducing the amounts that state Medicaid programs pay for generic drugs ($1 billion).

Modify Refundable Tax Credits. Under the President's proposals, various refundable tax credits would be modified. The President proposes to expand the earned income tax credit for workers without qualifying children. In addition, the lifetime learning credit and the AOTC would be consolidated into an expanded AOTC, and the refundable portion of that credit would increase. Those proposals, along with others that would affect the refundable portion of those credits and of the child tax credit, would increase outlays by $114 billion over the 2017–2026 period, according to JCT.[14]

Cancel Automatic Spending Reductions. Automatic reductions in mandatory spending (also known as sequestration) were put in place through 2021 by the Budget Control Act of 2011 and subsequently extended through 2025. The President proposes to cancel those reductions, beginning in 2017. If that happened, mandatory spending over the coming decade would be $113 billion higher than under current law, CBO estimates. Outlays for Medicare account for nearly 90 percent of that increase.

Other Proposals That Would Affect Mandatory Spending. Taken together, other proposals contained in the President's budget would, on net, increase mandatory outlays by $76 billion over the 2017–2026 period. The proposal with the largest effect on outlays ($57 billion) would create America Fast Forward Bonds as an optional alternative to certain tax-exempt bonds issued by state and local governments. That proposal would also increase revenues by $53 billion, resulting in a net increase in the deficit of $4 billion over the 2017–2026 period, according to JCT's estimates.

Proposals That Would Affect Discretionary Spending

CBO estimates that the President's proposals would result in discretionary outlays over the next decade that were $288 billion (or 2 percent) lower than those in the agency's baseline. That reduction would be the net result of three factors. First, funding for OCO—which is not constrained by the caps on discretionary spending originally established by the Budget Control Act of 2011— would be $619 billion less than the amounts projected in the baseline (which are based on the 2016 appropriation and adjusted for future inflation).[15] Second, $41 billion in discretionary spending for certain surface transportation programs would be reclassified as mandatory. Third, all other discretionary spending would be $372 billion (or 3 percent) higher under the President's proposed budget than in the baseline.

Discretionary outlays under the President's proposals would equal 6.3 percent of GDP in 2017 and fall to 4.9 percent by 2026; in CBO's baseline, they are 6.2 percent and 5.2 percent, respectively. They have never amounted to less than 6.0 percent of GDP in any year since 1962, the earliest year for which such data have been reported.

---

12. Under the rules governing baseline projections for expiring programs, CBO already projects funding for CHIP after 2017 at an annualized amount of about $6 billion. CBO estimates that fully funding the program for two years, as proposed by the President, would cost an additional $6 billion above the amounts projected in the baseline.

13. A medical loss ratio is the percentage of premium revenues that insurers spend on medical claims and certain related activities.

14. The proposals would also reduce revenues by $134 billion over the 2017–2026 period.

---

15. OCO funding requested for 2017 for the Department of Defense, as well as the corresponding total for 2016, includes some amounts that are intended to be used for non-OCO activities.

Table 4.

Discretionary Budget Authority Proposed by the President for 2016 and 2017, Compared With 2015 Appropriations

Billions of Dollars

	Actual, 2015	President's Proposals, 2016[a]	President's Budget, 2017[b]	Percentage Change	
				2015–2016	2016–2017
Defense					
Funding constrained by caps	521	548	552	5.1	0.7
Overseas contingency operations[c]	64	59	59	-8.7	**
Other adjustments to the caps	*	0	0	-100.0	n.a.
Subtotal	586	607	610	3.6	0.6
Nondefense					
Funding constrained by caps	507	537	538	5.9	0.3
Overseas contingency operations[c]	9	15	15	60.9	**
Other adjustments to the caps	13	11	11	-17.3	-4.5
Subtotal	530	563	564	6.2	0.2
Total	**1,116**	**1,170**	**1,174**	**4.8**	**0.4**

Source: Congressional Budget Office.

Estimates do not include obligation limitations for certain transportation programs. They also do not include enacted and proposed changes to certain mandatory programs through the appropriation process. In keeping with long-standing procedures, those changes are credited against discretionary spending for purposes of budget enforcement.

n.a. = not applicable; * = between zero and $500 million; ** = between -0.05 percent and zero.

a. The President's proposed changes to enacted appropriations for 2016 consist of a supplemental request for funding of $1.8 billion to prepare for and respond to the spread of the Zika virus. That request contains $0.2 billion in mandatory spending that is not included in this table.

b. Excludes proposed reductions of $21 billion in budget authority for certain mandatory programs through the appropriation process.

c. Overseas contingency operations consist of military operations and related activities in Afghanistan and elsewhere.

Supplemental Appropriations for 2016. Appropriations for 2016 would be slightly higher under the President's proposals than in CBO's baseline. That is because the Administration is requesting $1.8 billion in supplemental funding to respond to the Zika virus.

Proposed Appropriations for 2017. The President has requested a total of $1.15 trillion in appropriations for 2017. That amount includes certain proposed reductions in mandatory budget authority that would be enacted in appropriation bills; according to long-standing procedures, such changes in mandatory budget authority are counted as reductions in discretionary funding in the enforcement of budget rules. Excluding those reductions (which total $21 billion), the proposed appropriations for 2017 would be $1.17 trillion (see Table 4).[16] That amount is $4 billion (or 0.4 percent) more than the amount (like-wise excluding offsets for changes to mandatory funding) that has been appropriated, or requested by the Administration as supplemental appropriations, for 2016. The request for 2017 would maintain the caps on discretionary

spending in their current form—that is, as they were modified by the Bipartisan Budget Act of 2015.

For defense discretionary programs in 2017, the President proposes appropriations of $610 billion, $3.6 billion (or 0.6 percent) more than has been provided in 2016. That proposal comprises $59 billion for defense-related OCO—the same amount appropriated for 2016—and $552 billion for other defense activities, about the current limit set by law for 2017. For those non-OCO defense activities, the proposed amount is $4 billion (or 0.7 percent)

---

16. Two sources account for most of the proposed reduction in mandatory budget authority in appropriation bills. The largest would be a limit on the Department of Justice's ability to obligate balances from the Crime Victims Fund—as typically occurs in appropriation bills—which would reduce funding by $10.5 billion in 2017 and increase it by the same amount in 2018. The second source is a proposed cancellation of $6 billion in funding for CHIP in 2017. All such reductions in mandatory funding would be in nondefense programs.

more than the 2016 appropriations. The increases would be concentrated in operation and maintenance ($8 billion) and research and development ($3 billion), and other categories of defense spending would receive increases totaling $2 billion. The increases would be partially offset by decreases in procurement ($8 billion) and military construction ($1 billion).

For nondefense discretionary programs in 2017, the President proposes appropriations of $564 billion, not counting the $21 billion in proposed changes to mandatory programs enacted in appropriation bills. That $564 billion is about $1 billion (or 0.2 percent) more than has been appropriated or requested for 2016. The largest increases would be in funding for hospital and medical care for veterans, which would be $3.1 billion (or 4.9 percent) higher than in 2016, and in funding for education, job training, and social services, which would be $2.6 billion (or 2.7 percent) higher. In the other direction, the largest decline would be in funding for surface transportation programs, which would fall by $4.4 billion, primarily because of the reclassification of some of those programs as mandatory.

Total funding for nondefense discretionary activities that is not constrained by the spending caps—for nondefense OCO, certain disaster assistance efforts, program integrity initiatives, and emergencies—would remain at or near the amount provided for 2016.

Proposed Appropriations for 2018 Through 2026. For 2018, the President proposes appropriations that are $4 billion lower than those proposed for 2017—the net result of a reduction in OCO funding and an increase in other discretionary funding that would be accomplished by raising the caps higher than they are under current law:

■ Funding for OCO would fall by $63 billion, to $11 billion (about one-sixth of the amount requested for 2017);

■ Funding for defense programs other than OCO would increase by $33 billion (or 5.9 percent); and

■ Funding for nondefense programs other than OCO would increase by $26 billion (or 4.9 percent).

After 2018, appropriations would increase by an average of 1.8 percent per year—from $1.15 trillion in 2018 to $1.32 trillion in 2026. Broad funding policies would include the following:

■ Increasing the caps on budget authority through 2021 above the levels under current law;

■ Extending the caps through 2026; and

■ Maintaining funding for OCO at $11 billion per year through 2021 and eliminating it thereafter.

Outlays for discretionary programs under the President's proposals would be $2 billion higher than in CBO's baseline in 2018, but lower than in the baseline in every year thereafter. By 2026, such outlays would be $68 billion (or 4.7 percent) below the amount projected in the baseline; excluding OCO funding, they would be $19 billion (or 1.4 percent) more than the amount projected in the baseline.

Effects on Net Interest

The President's proposals would reduce the government's borrowing needs by $2.1 trillion over the 2016–2026 period, CBO estimates.[17] As a result, net interest costs for the period would be $343 billion lower than they are projected to be in the baseline. In 2026, net interest costs under the President's budget would amount to 2.8 percent of GDP—less than the 3.0 percent in CBO's baseline projections for that year, but double CBO's estimate for 2016, mostly because interest rates are expected to be much higher than they have been recently.

Differences Between CBO's and the Administration's Estimates of the President's Budget

CBO's estimates of the deficit under the President's budget are smaller than the Administration's estimates through 2019 but greater between 2020 and 2026 (see Table 5). Some of the differences result from the fact that CBO and the Administration use different economic forecasts—that is, projections of GDP, interest rates, inflation factors, the unemployment rate, and other economic variables. That difference, in turn, arises in part because the Administration incorporates its assessment of the economic effects

---

17. The change in the government's borrowing needs ($2.3 trillion over the 10-year period) differs from the amount of deficit reduction under the President's budget ($2.4 trillion) because the borrowing needs include the effects of proposals that affect the cash flows for credit programs; the federal budget shows the subsidy costs of those programs, not the annual cash flows. The most significant effects on such cash flows from the President's policies stem from proposals related to student loans and credit programs for infrastructure.

Table 5.

Sources of Differences Between CBO's and the Administration's Estimates of the President's Budget

Billions of Dollars

	2016	2017	2018	2019	2020	2021	2022	2023	2024	2025	2026	Total 2017-2021	Total 2017-2026
						Administration's Estimate							
Deficit Under the President's Budget	-616	-503	-454	-549	-534	-552	-660	-677	-650	-741	-793	-2,593	-6,113
					Differences Between CBO's and the Administration's Estimates								
Differences in Revenues[a]													
Legislative	*	*	*	*	*	*	*	*	*	*	0	*	*
Economic	41	52	38	1	-32	-59	-83	-105	-127	-149	-177	-1	-642
Technical	-7	-24	-65	-61	-108	-135	-132	-131	-130	-107	-97	-394	-990
Total, Revenues	**33**	**28**	**-28**	**-60**	**-140**	**-195**	**-215**	**-236**	**-257**	**-256**	**-274**	**-394**	**-1,632**
Differences in Outlays[b]													
Mandatory													
Legislative	0	0	0	0	0	0	0	0	0	*	0	0	*
Economic	-1	-4	*	8	14	14	13	11	9	6	15	32	86
Technical	-39	-26	-62	-60	-61	-68	-70	-72	-78	-72	-99	-277	-668
Subtotal, mandatory	-40	-30	-62	-52	-47	-54	-57	-61	-69	-66	-84	-245	-582
Discretionary (Technical)	-27	-13	-12	-4	-2	3	17	14	8	14	13	-29	37
Net interest													
Legislative	*	*	*	*	*	*	*	*	*	*	*	*	*
Economic	-4	-10	-14	-19	-23	-27	-28	-26	-20	-15	-10	-93	-192
Technical	17	12	-10	-15	-19	-17	-16	-14	-12	-12	-15	-50	-118
Subtotal, net interest	12	2	-24	-34	-41	-44	-44	-39	-32	-27	-25	-142	-311
Total, Outlays	**-54**	**-42**	**-98**	**-90**	**-90**	**-96**	**-84**	**-87**	**-94**	**-80**	**-96**	**-416**	**-856**
Total Differences[a]	**87**	**70**	**70**	**31**	**-51**	**-99**	**-131**	**-149**	**-163**	**-176**	**-178**	**22**	**-776**
							CBO's Estimate						
Deficit Under the President's Budget	-529	-433	-383	-518	-585	-651	-791	-826	-813	-917	-972	-2,571	-6,889
Memorandum:													
Total Legislative Differences[a]	*	*	*	*	*	*	*	*	*	*	*	*	*
Total Economic Differences[a]	46	66	52	12	-23	-46	-69	-90	-116	-140	-182	60	-536
Total Technical Differences[a]	42	4	18	19	-27	-53	-63	-59	-47	-37	4	-38	-241

Sources: Congressional Budget Office; staff of the Joint Committee on Taxation.

* = between -$500 million and $500 million.

a. Positive numbers indicate that such differences make CBO's estimate of the deficit smaller than the Administration's estimate.

b. Positive numbers indicate that such differences make CBO's estimate of the deficit larger than the Administration's estimate.

that the President's proposals would have, whereas CBO uses the same economic projections that it did for its March 2016 baseline, aside from incorporating the effects of the President's proposed immigration reform on the population and the labor force. (CBO will incorporate the other economic effects of the President's proposals in a subsequent report.) The remaining differences between CBO's and the Administration's estimates result from

technical estimating differences, such as differences in how CBO and the Administration incorporate demographic, historical, and other data into projections.

CBO's estimate of the 2016 deficit under the President's budget is $87 billion lower than the Administration's estimate; that is because CBO's estimate of revenues is $33 billion higher and its estimate of outlays $54 billion lower. Looking farther ahead, CBO estimates higher revenues under the President's budget than the Administration does in 2017, but lower ones from 2018 through 2026. In every year of the 2017–2026 period, CBO estimates lower outlays under the President's budget than the Administration does. Taking all of those pieces together, CBO estimates a cumulative deficit for the 2017–2026 period that is $776 billion higher than the Administration's estimate.

Differences in Estimates of Revenues

For 2016, CBO's estimate of revenues under the President's budget is $33 billion higher than the Administration's. Differences between CBO's and the Administration's economic forecasts account for a difference of $41 billion; the most significant factor is that CBO expects higher wages and salaries, and thus a larger tax base for individual income taxes and payroll taxes, than the Administration does. Some technical factors partly offset that $41 billion, reducing CBO's estimate of revenues by $7 billion in relation to the Administration's.

For 2017 through 2026, CBO projects that revenues under the President's budget would total $1.6 trillion (or 3.5 percent) less than the Administration estimates. CBO attributes $1.0 trillion of that difference to the following technical factors, which include both the estimated effects of the President's proposals and CBO's projections under current law:

■ CBO and JCT project that the President's proposals would raise revenues over the next decade by $585 billion less than the Administration estimates. The largest components of that difference relate to the President's proposals to impose a onetime tax on certain foreign earnings ($105 billion) and to limit the extent to which deductions and exclusions would reduce tax liability for higher-income taxpayers ($103 billion).

■ In addition, CBO projects that revenues during the next decade under current law will be $406 billion lower than the Administration projects. That difference largely reflects CBO's lower estimate of the effective payroll tax rate on wages and salaries.

The remaining difference between CBO's and the Administration's revenue projections over the decade, $642 billion, results from differences in baseline economic forecasts—largely CBO's lower projection of corporate profits.

Differences in Estimates of Outlays

For 2016, CBO estimates lower outlays under the President's budget than the Administration does. The same is true for each year of the 2017–2026 period, with differences ranging between $42 billion and $98 billion. Over the decade as a whole, CBO's estimates of outlays under the President's budget are therefore lower than the Administration's—by $856 billion, or 1.6 percent.

Differences for 2016. CBO's estimate of mandatory spending this year under the President's budget is $40 billion lower than the Administration's estimate. A third of that difference ($13 billion) arises because CBO estimates a smaller number of Social Security beneficiaries and therefore lower Social Security spending. An additional $8 billion of the difference arises from CBO's lower estimate of outlays for income security programs, particularly unemployment compensation, the Supplemental Nutrition Assistance Program, and mortgage modifications under the Troubled Asset Relief Program. CBO's lower estimate of outlays for student loans accounts for $4 billion of the difference. And another $4 billion arises from CBO's assumption that the President's proposed classification of certain transportation outlays as mandatory would begin to apply in 2017—rather than in 2016, as the Administration assumes.

CBO's estimate of discretionary outlays in 2016 under the President's budget is $27 billion lower than the Administration's. CBO anticipates lower outlays in a variety of areas; the largest of those differences are in defense ($8 billion), community and regional development ($6 billion), and international affairs, health, and education and social services ($3 billion each). However, CBO's assumption that the proposal to reclassify transportation outlays would begin next year, rather than this year, pushes CBO's estimate of discretionary outlays up by $4 billion.

CBO estimates that net interest costs this year will be $12 billion more than the total reported by the Administration. That variation stems mostly from differences in expectations about the timing and maturity structure of Treasury borrowing.

Differences for 2017 Through 2026. Over 10 years, CBO's estimates are lower than the Administration's for mandatory spending (by $582 billion), higher for discretionary spending (by $37 billion), and lower for outlays for net interest (by $311 billion).

Mandatory Spending. Technical factors account for most of the differences between CBO's and the Administration's estimates of mandatory spending under the President's budget. Such factors push CBO's estimates below those of the Administration by $668 billion over the 2017–2026 period. CBO's estimates are the farthest below the Administration's for the following categories of spending:

■ Spending to subsidize health insurance and to stabilize premiums in the marketplaces established by the Affordable Care Act ($350 billion), mostly because CBO's estimates of enrollment and per-person costs are lower;

■ Social Security outlays ($254 billion), primarily because CBO expects fewer people to collect Old-Age and Survivors Insurance benefits;

■ Veterans' disability compensation benefits ($101 billion), because CBO expects caseloads and average benefits to grow more slowly; and

■ Medicare spending ($65 billion), chiefly because the Administration anticipates more rapid growth in spending per beneficiary.

Some technical estimating differences go in the opposite direction, pushing CBO's estimates for the 10-year period higher than the Administration's. The largest differences are for these categories of spending:

■ Outlays related to Fannie Mae and Freddie Mac ($183 billion), primarily because CBO's projections are estimates of the anticipated subsidy costs for new mortgage guarantees issued by those two entities, whereas the Administration's projections reflect estimated net cash payments and receipts;[18] and

■ Medicaid spending ($170 billion), primarily because of different estimates of per-person costs and enrollment.

Partly offsetting those technical factors are economic ones that push up CBO's projections of mandatory spending under the President's budget, in relation to the Administration's projections, by an estimated $86 billion over the 2017–2026 period. The most significant effects can be seen in CBO's projection of outlays for Social Security, which are boosted by $103 billion—primarily because

CBO generally expects higher inflation, as measured by the consumer price index for urban wage earners and clerical workers, and therefore larger cost-of-living adjustments to Social Security benefits. Conversely, CBO's estimate of Medicare spending over the decade is $62 billion lower than the Administration's, because CBO generally expects lower inflation for medical services.

Discretionary Spending. CBO's estimate of discretionary spending under the President's budget during the 2017–2026 period exceeds the Administration's by $37 billion. The largest differences involve Pell grants ($26 billion higher, according to CBO) and the subsidies for mortgage credit programs administered by the Federal Housing Administration ($43 billion higher). However, CBO's estimates of outlays are lower, in total, for other discretionary programs, in part because the agency projects $12 billion less in defense spending under the President's proposals than the Administration does.

Net Interest. Finally, CBO's estimate of net outlays for interest under the President's budget is $311 billion (or 5.4 percent) lower than the Administration's estimate for the 2017–2026 period. Interest rates are generally lower in CBO's forecast than in the Administration's; as a result of that economic factor, interest costs are $192 billion lower in CBO's projection than in the Administration's. The remaining $118 billion difference between the two estimates of interest costs results from technical factors—primarily different expectations about the mix of securities that the Treasury will issue over the next 10 years.

---

18. The Administration treats Fannie Mae and Freddie Mac as non-governmental organizations and records payments between the Treasury and the two entities on a cash basis. CBO, however, projects the budgetary impact of the two entities' operations in future years as if they were being conducted by a federal agency because of the degree of management and financial control that the government exercises over them. CBO therefore estimates the net lifetime costs—that is, the subsidy costs adjusted for market risk—of the guarantees that those entities will issue and of the loans that they will hold and shows those costs as federal outlays in the year of issuance. However, to provide CBO's best estimate of what the Treasury will ultimately report as the federal deficit for 2016, CBO's baseline includes an estimate of the cash receipts from the two entities to the Treasury for this year. See Congressional Budget Office, *CBO's Budgetary Treatment of Fannie Mae and Freddie Mac* (January 2010), www.cbo.gov/publication/41887, and *Fannie Mae, Freddie Mac, and the Federal Role in the Secondary Mortgage Market* (December 2010), www.cbo.gov/publication/21992.

About This Document

The Congressional Budget Office prepared this analysis of the President's budgetary proposals for fiscal year 2017 at the request of the Senate Committee on Appropriations. In keeping with CBO's mandate to provide objective, impartial analysis, the report makes no recommendations.

Christina Hawley Anthony and Meredith Decker of CBO's Budget Analysis Division wrote the report, with assistance from Mark Booth and Pamela Greene and under the guidance of Theresa Gullo, Holly Harvey, Jeffrey Holland, H. Samuel Papenfuss, and David Weiner. The estimates described here were the work of many analysts at CBO and on the staff of the Joint Committee on Taxation.

Robert Sunshine and Wendy Edelberg reviewed the report. Benjamin Plotinsky edited it, with assistance from Gabe Waggoner, and Jeanine Rees prepared it for publication. An electronic version is available on CBO's website (www.cbo.gov/publication/51383).

Keith Hall
Director

March 2016